# Landscape
# Gardening

# Landscape Gardening

**WRITER**
PHILIP HARDGRAVE

**PHOTOGRAPHER**
STEFAN HAMES

**ILLUSTRATORS**
PETE COLLINS
LUCY SARGEANT
LOIS LOVEJOY

**LAWN & GARDEN**

Acquisition, Development and Production Services by
BMR, Corte Madera, CA

Acquisition: JACK JENNINGS, BOB DOLEZAL

Series Concept: BOB DOLEZAL

Developmental Editing: BOB DOLEZAL

Photographic Director: ALAN COPELAND

Cover Design: KAREN EMERSON

Cover Photo: JIM GALLOP

Interior Art: PETE COLLINS

North American Map: RON HILDEBRAND

Copy Editing: NAOMI LUCKS, JANET REED

Proofreader: TOM HASSETT

Typography and Page Layout: BARBARA GELFAND

Index: SYLVIA COATES

Horticulturist and Site Scout: PEGGY HENRY

Color Separations: PREPRESS ASSEMBLY INCORPORATED

Printing and Binding: PENDELL PRINTING INC.

Production Management: THOMAS E. DORSANEO,
    JANE RYAN

Film: FUJI VELVIA

**Library of Congress Catalog-in-Publication Data**
Hardgrave, Philip.
    Landscape gardening / writer, Philip Hardgrave;
photographer, Stefan Hames; illustrators, Peter
Collins, Lucy Sargeant, Lois Lovejoy.
        p. cm.
    Includes index.
    ISBN: 1-880281-02-3
    1. Landscape gardening. 2. Plants, Ornamental.
I. Title.
[SB473.H356 1992]
712—dc20
                                              92-26413
                                              CIP

Special thanks to Strybing Arboretum & Botanical
Gardens, Golden Gate Park, San Francisco, CA;
University of California Botanical Garden, Berkeley,
CA; The Davis Arboretum, University of California,
Davis, CA; The Dry Garden, Berkeley, CA; Petri's
Restaurant, Napa, CA; Mudd's Restaurant, San Ramon,
CA; Mary Jobson, Sonoma, CA; Jerry Cichon, Sonoma,
CA; Mr. & Mrs. Rankin, Santa Rosa, CA; Dick Turner,
San Francisco, CA.

Additional photo credits: Kim Newton and Robert
Frerck, Woodfin Camp & Associates, pages 8–9, for
Spanish/Moorish and Formal Gardens. Bonnie Lee
Appleton, page 36, for Fountaingrass. Robert Lyons,
pages 36, 51, for Reedgrass, Dogwood. Michael Landis,
pages 54, 63, for Azalea, Ice Plant. Derek Fell, pages
51–63, for Camellia, Lilac, Rhododendron, Sorbus,
Japanese Yew, Redbud, Callery Pear, Yucca. Arizona-
Sonora Desert Museum, pages 62–63, for Suguaro.
Saxon Holt, page 55, Golden Yew.

92    93    94    95    10    9    8    7    6    5    4    3    2

# LANDSCAPE GARDENING

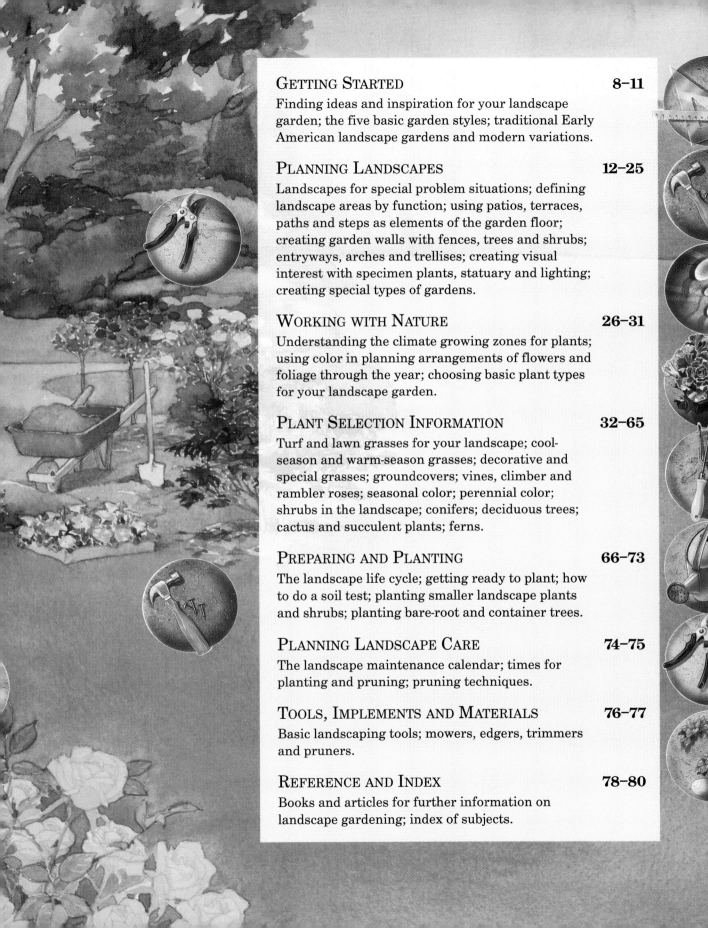

# COMPARING LANDSCAPES

Landscape ideas and designs can be found in garden magazines, coffee-table books or even in the paintings of landscape artists. Viewing public and private gardens in your own area, and consulting with landscaping professionals, will help you choose the landscape plan that is best for you.

Natural—
Native plants in planned settings

Spanish and Moorish—
repeating patterns.

Oriental—
need most care and strict design.

8

# BASIC GARDEN STYLES

Planning a landscape garden begins with gathering ideas and insights from every source of garden designs, then working up a plan that includes the elements you wish to use in your site. Sitting down to draw up a garden plan may seem too much like homework, especially if you enjoy just putting plants out, but you will obtain more satisfying results if you design your landscape carefully. Every tree, shrub and plant has a unique color, shape, volume, texture and size; successful landscapes combine them into a pleasing and harmonious design.

You can draw inspiration from the five basic styles that garden planners around the world have developed over the years. The *Formal* Italian or French garden is regular and geometric, with every plant, tree and shrub fitted into an orderly, structured design. The *English* or country garden is a more informal style, but it requires a well-thought-out arrangement of massed shrubs, bunched flowers, and gently curving lines to create an unplanned, natural appearance. *Oriental* gardens rely upon the careful placement of trees, plants, water and stones to develop evocative themes for the viewer's enjoyment; the best Japanese and East Asian gardens skillfully balance informal, natural elements with subtle, asymmetrical patterns that avoid repetition or predictability. In contrast, *Islamic* courtyard gardens display the Moorish-Spanish tradition of repeated geometric patterns, pastel colors and shading to provide relief from harsh sunlight, usually incorporating fountains or pools into the plan. *Native* or low-maintenance natural gardens try to use only naturally-occurring plants and existing topography to create the effect of wildness in a garden setting.

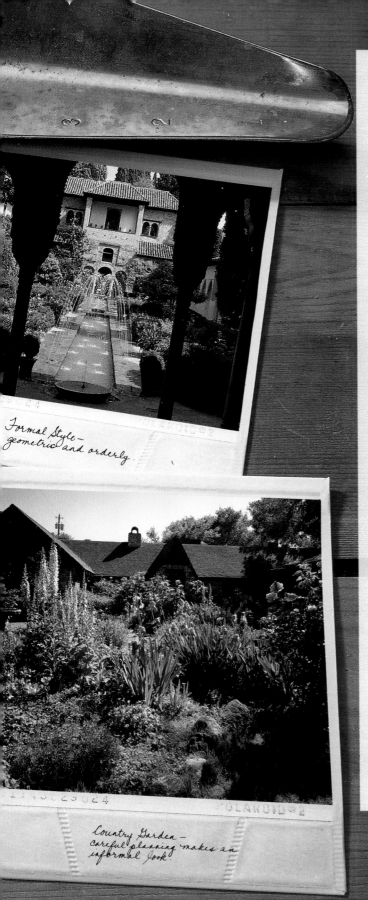

Formal Style—
geometric and orderly.

Country Garden—
careful planning makes an
informal look.

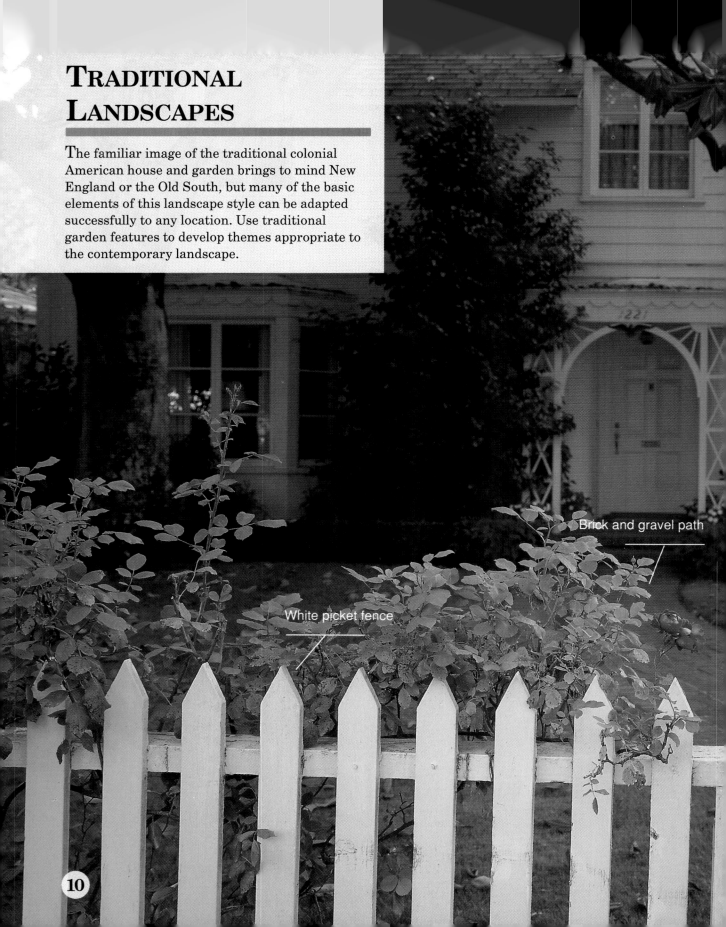

# TRADITIONAL LANDSCAPES

The familiar image of the traditional colonial American house and garden brings to mind New England or the Old South, but many of the basic elements of this landscape style can be adapted successfully to any location. Use traditional garden features to develop themes appropriate to the contemporary landscape.

Brick and gravel path

White picket fence

Shade tree

Low hedge

## THE TRADITIONAL APPROACH

Early American or colonial-style houses featured both functional and decorative gardens arranged in formal, symmetrical patterns around the residence. Typically, an ornamental "parterre" garden in a formal pattern was bordered by low hedges, enclosing ornamental flower beds or small shaped shrubs within a geometrical brick or gravel walkway. The herb garden near the kitchen and the fruit orchard to the side or rear of the house were set off from the ornamental garden. The traditional white picket fence faced the road and divided the main areas of the gardens.

This formal colonial style gave way to a more informal style, introducing natural elements of the country garden to the domestic landscape. Well-groomed lawns, massed flowers and shrubs set in planting beds along gravel paths, and large shade trees were added to the traditional garden. The white picket fence defined the borders of the garden, the walkways and the property as a whole.

Today, these are still in use in many parts of the country. The colonial style of architecture remains very popular throughout the eastern United States. The designer working in this style can draw upon traditional features by using antique garden furniture, flower borders and traditional plants such as boxwood, privet, honeysuckle and periwinkle. Although few landscapers today would choose a parterre garden with white picket fences unless it blended well with the local architecture, landscape elements from more recent periods are often mixed with colonial themes. The cottage garden of the Victorian era, the herb garden of the colonial period and the formal garden of the European tradition can all be used as sources for gardens with traditional themes.

# LANDSCAPES FOR SPECIAL SITUATIONS

Not all yards and landscapes are well-suited to the traditional front and side yard arrangement. If you have little or no lawn area, a hilly terrain, or need space for a swimming pool or for children at play, you will have to adapt your landscape plan to fit these conditions.

**Limited Space**
If you don't have a large yard, make maximum use of the space you have, eliminating elements that don't fit easily.

**Hillside Yard**
Landscaping a hillside lot can require careful use of terracing, retaining walls, and other structures, or it may simply call for a spreading groundcover.

**Play Yard**
Play areas should have childproof plants without sharp branches or leaves; chipped bark or heavy-wear grasses make durable and attractive surfaces for playing children.

**Pool Landscape**
Creative use of plants and shrubs will enable you to design your pool area for privacy and safety, and can help to hide unsightly pool pumps and other equipment.

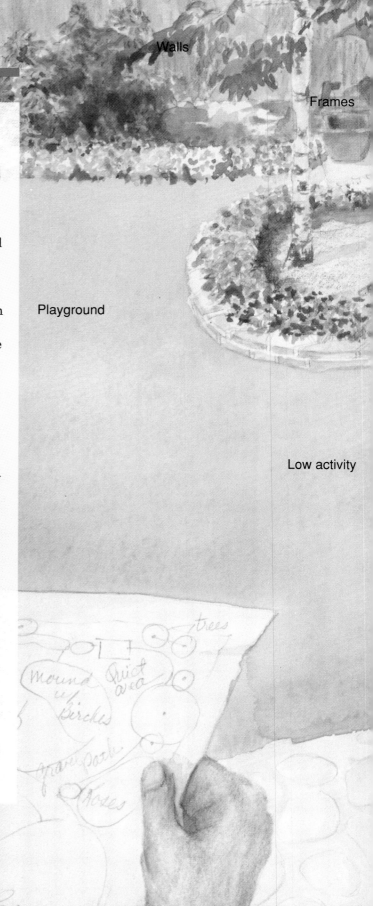

# DEFINING AREAS

## THINKING ABOUT LANDSCAPES

Drawing a landscape plan to fit your lifestyle involves much more than deciding which plants you want. Take the following into account: houses, driveways, work and play areas, neighboring properties and the special demands imposed by swimming pools, ball courts, and decks or terraces. A landscape only becomes usable when it can be appreciated by walking through, sitting down and looking at it in comfort. All areas should be designed for the active enjoyment of those who will actually use the garden.

Different areas of the landscape receive different amounts of use, of course. Begin by defining different areas of the garden in terms of access points, activities and functional purposes. Then you'll know which spots will receive heavier use, and which can be reserved for decorative elements and view points. Area planning means drawing a measured overhead plan showing the location of all structures, fences, walls, trees, shrubs, paths and steps, then taking photographs from each entry point and view area to help visualize the final effect after planting.

Plan your landscape garden in three dimensions. Try sketching eye-level views from the most-used areas, working from your photographs. Remember that the size of the trees and shrubs will change as they mature, altering the scale and balance of your plantings with respect to each other and to the structures around them. Design your garden for optimum visibility from the garden floor and the house, and for privacy and seclusion from neighboring houses and yards.

Walls

Frames

Playground

Low activity

Occasional
activity

Garden
viewing

Floor

Frequent activity

15

# PATIOS, TERRACES, PATHS AND STEPS

When planning the landscape, keep in mind the many options for paving its "floors"—brick, stone, concrete, wood, chips and gravel. Each has its own distinctive texture and form, and each is best suited for a particular need. Choose materials for their use as well as for appearance—non-skid surfaces for safety in wet areas; chipped bark or wood chips to soften play areas; durable stone, brick or concrete for areas that will receive heavy traffic. Always grade and level walkways carefully to prevent hazard from uneven surfaces. Installing proper drainage will insure that any surface water runs off without puddling.

**Smooth Textures**
Choose brick, marble, tile, concrete or wood for a flat, low-maintenance surface.

**Rough Textures**
Provide variety with crushed gravel, river pebbles, cobblestones, chips or fieldstones.

**Pathways**
Winding garden paths suggest other vistas and expand space.

**Changing Levels**
Steps leading up or down provide easy access and help define uses.

# ENTERING THE LANDSCAPE

Entryways and walkways define our views of the landscape, so they should be designed to make the best possible impression. Entries and paths also provide access to different areas of the garden for everyday maintenance. Stepping stones and walkways should be made of stable, non-skid materials for sure footing. Brick, pea-gravel, and shredded bark all create attractive textures and patterns for the garden floor.

The purpose of the garden path is to allow one or two persons to walk through in comfort, so pathways should be at least 3 ft. wide—4–5 ft. for two people to walk side-by-side. Remember to leave a buffer area along the side of the path where hedges, tree limbs or shrubs protrude.

The garden path should rarely be straight and narrow; varying the curve and width of the walkway creates a greater variety of perspectives. Gently curving paths can level out steeper climbs and present new, unexpected views of the garden. Sharp intersections and tight curves will feel uncomfortable, just like sharp rocks and unstable surfaces. Flower borders and hedges provide a sense of security where the pedestrian's footing is unsure.

Where the pathway cannot be conveniently curved to go around a slope, use wooden, stone or brick steps to adjust the level of the path to the new height. Steps should come in uniform series, with risers of 4–6 in. and treads of 12–18 in.—the lower the riser, the deeper the tread and vice-versa. Make the steps wider than the path, and give the treads a slight forward slope for drainage. For shallower grades, use longer ramps with timber risers and earthen treads; steeper steps may require landings or handrails.

Like walkways, steps and stairways benefit from decorative borders. An attractively bordered set of weathered flagstone or timber steps can be a decorative feature in its own right.

# Walls, Fences, Trees and Shrubs

Garden walls define the boundaries of the landscape, but they also serve many functional and decorative purposes. Use fences or walls as supports and backdrops for greenery that will screen and shade the garden interior. These structures will connect and unify plantings throughout the garden.

## Walls

Low- or medium-height walls can serve as borders, structural supports and retaining barriers; they can also be used as seats or freestanding elements in the garden. Whether using brick, timber, or mortared or dry stone, make sure the wall has solid footings and good drainage.

## Fences

Solid wood fences offer security and create boundaries; open and semitransparent fences can also be used for pool barriers, planting barriers and decorative screens. Gates and screens should be made in a style and material suited to the design of the garden areas they enclose.

18

## OUTDOOR SPACES

Think of your garden as an outdoor room with walls made of living plants. The trees provide protection from the wind as well as shade from the sun. Closely planted evergreens, such as spruces, grow together into a solid screen for privacy; shrubs form low hedges and borders. Fast-growing vines climb over fences to create walls of foliage. Decorative plants, fences and structures all help create a sense of enclosed space.

Landscape trees and shrubs come in a wide variety of shapes and sizes, but they can be thought of in terms of their basic forms. Vertical trees, such as the Italian cypress, are upright pillars. Rounded trees spread their branches out into spheres. Many conifers form pyramidal shapes, but some branch out into irregular horizontal forms. Shrubs also come in all varieties of upright, conical, rounded and horizontal shapes. Placed in a balanced, rhythmic landscape composition, trees and shrubs will lend variety to the simplest outdoor space.

The outdoor room has a much higher ceiling and larger floor space than a small interior room, so you should place your trees and shrubs with a feeling for the scale of the landscape. Smaller plants and shrubs belong in the foreground, while larger shrubs and trees should form the background, to create a sense of distance and perspective that feels natural for the size of your garden.

**Trees and Shrubs**
To create natural barriers and define the visual space of the garden, trees and shrubs can be planted in regular patterns around the perimeter of the garden. This wall of trees will enhance privacy and create a foliage backdrop for smaller garden plants.

**19**

# ENTRIES AND OVERHEADS

The entry to the landscape garden should welcome the visitor, either through the formal design of a gate, door or archway, or through the informal arrangement of a trellis or plant-covered arch. Breaks in walls, screens and hedges also create inviting transitions between garden areas.

### Overhead Structures
Overhead structures provide seasonal shade for central areas of the landscape. Climbing vines and shrubs lend an ornamental touch to the structures.

### Tree Canopies
Mature trees provide shade and shelter, filtering the sun and creating varied patterns of light and dark.

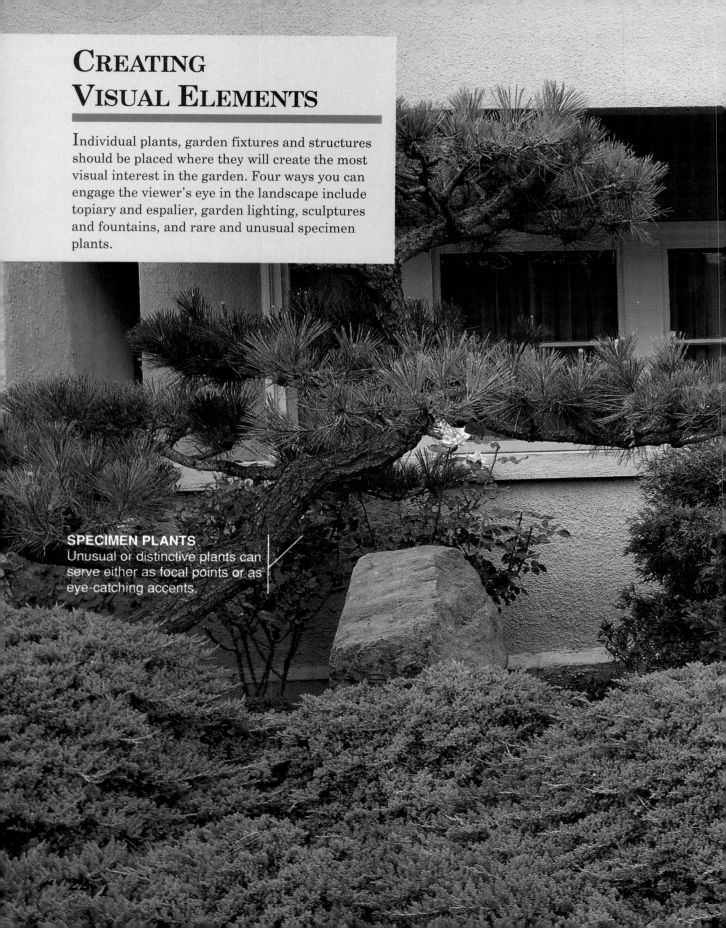

# CREATING VISUAL ELEMENTS

Individual plants, garden fixtures and structures should be placed where they will create the most visual interest in the garden. Four ways you can engage the viewer's eye in the landscape include topiary and espalier, garden lighting, sculptures and fountains, and rare and unusual specimen plants.

**SPECIMEN PLANTS**
Unusual or distinctive plants can serve either as focal points or as eye-catching accents.

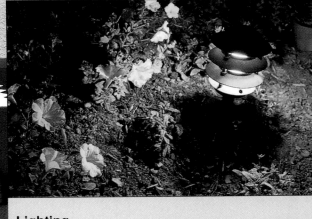

## Topiary and Espalier
Create living designs by training plants on a framework of wood or wire set against a wall or fence to outline its form.

Topiary plants are trained and pruned into ornamental figures.

## Lighting
Nighttime viewing of your landscape garden can be dramatically enhanced with accent lighting.

## Statues, fountains and sculptures
Statuary can provide dramatic emphasis of a garden theme. Bring moving water into the garden, whether in a fountain, waterfall or stream.

# SPECIAL GARDENS IN THE LANDSCAPE

Special "gardens within gardens" draw attention by mood, form and pattern, or clusters of color. For example, Japanese gardens are places of peaceful tranquility and rock gardens catch your eye. Shady nooks, with plants that prefer indirect sunlight, relieve the soul with their coolness and quiet.

**Landscape Flower Border**
The English flower border is a tradition for both country and cottage gardens, creating natural edgings with masses of color and a variety of plants.

## FORMAL ROSE GARDEN

A raised bed of roses can be a feature within the landscape, or a special garden unto itself. Provide ample footpaths and access points for close-up viewing of the roses.

### Hillside Features

Create berms and small hills to separate planting areas and to enclose flower beds of seasonal color.

### Groves and Miniature Forests

By clustering plantings of specimen trees and shrubs, you can create the effect of a woodland grove or miniature forest in a small area.

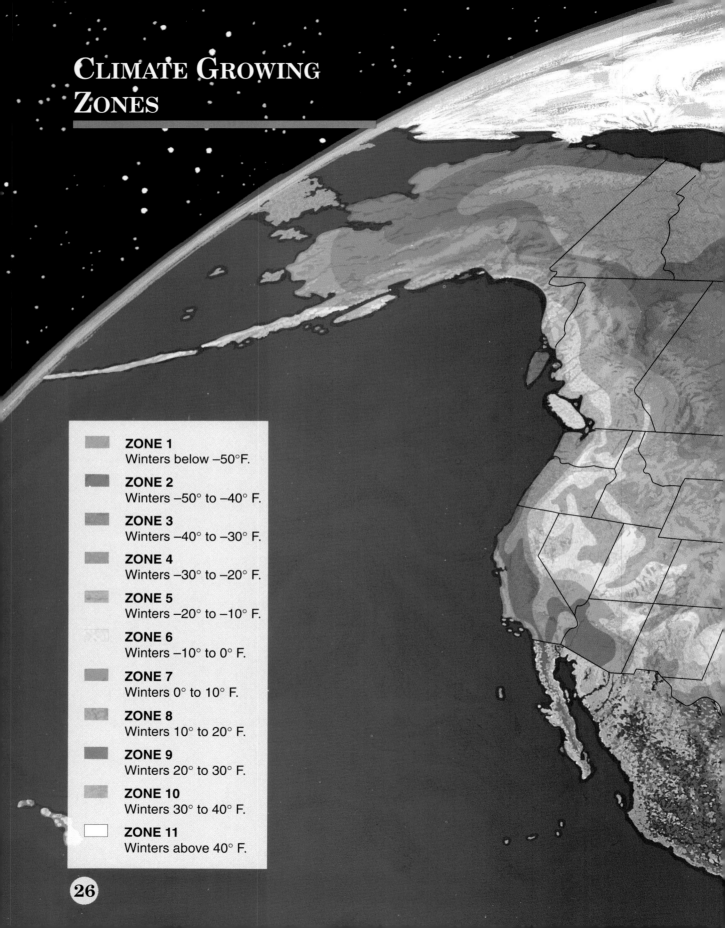

# CLIMATE GROWING ZONES

**ZONE 1**
Winters below −50°F.

**ZONE 2**
Winters −50° to −40° F.

**ZONE 3**
Winters −40° to −30° F.

**ZONE 4**
Winters −30° to −20° F.

**ZONE 5**
Winters −20° to −10° F.

**ZONE 6**
Winters −10° to 0° F.

**ZONE 7**
Winters 0° to 10° F.

**ZONE 8**
Winters 10° to 20° F.

**ZONE 9**
Winters 20° to 30° F.

**ZONE 10**
Winters 30° to 40° F.

**ZONE 11**
Winters above 40° F.

# PLANT HARDINESS

The hardiness of plants is their ability to thrive in particular climates. Hardiness is influenced by such factors as humidity of the air, number of days of sun, annual moisture, seasonal temperature variations and soil type. The degree of winter cold is probably the most important single factor affecting the ability of a plant to do well in a given climate.

The U.S. Department of Agriculture has divided the continent into geographic zones, numbered 1-11. They link places that share average annual minimum temperatures. Each plant is best adapted to one or more of these zones.

To use the map, locate your area on the map and note the zone which describes it. A description is given for each zone color. Remember, the *actual* minimum temperature in your garden may vary quite a bit from the zone for your area—it's *microclimate* is affected by hills and valleys, exposure and shading. If in doubt, ask your local Agricultural Extension Service for advice.

And remember: some plants *need* winter temperatures to dip below certain levels in order to thrive, while others do well anywhere south of their coldest tolerated climate zone.

# COLOR IN THE GARDEN

Yellows

Pinks

Reds

Multicolors

**Foliage Color**
Choose foliage plantings to emphasize or subdue
nearby annuals, perennials and bulb plantings.

28

Whites

Violets

**Seasonal Color**
Create striking garden accents with color spots;
some will bloom in autumn, others in spring or
summer. Colorful bark creates winter interest.

# CHOOSING GARDEN COLOR

Gardeners use color in their gardens as artists use paint from their palettes. Color can be found anywhere in the garden: tree bark, foliage, flowers, turf, bricks, stones or structures. Take care to choose only those colors that you wish to see, and to use them in ways that work together as the seasons change.

The color wheel will help you choose between the bright, primary colors—red, yellow and blue—and their softer complements—green, purple and orange. Hues closer together on the color wheel match appealingly, while those that are opposite each other clash with eye-dazzling contrast. Cool colors such as green and blue are more restful and appear to recede from the warmer, livelier colors—red, yellow, pink and orange.

Use these chromatic combinations in selecting garden colors. Choose a quiet, cool background of evergreen shrubs to emphasize bright red and yellow spring flowers. By the time nearby color-packed foliage trees turn, these flowers will be gone, but green foliage will still be there, making a maple tree's display of fall color all the more eye-catching. Even in winter, evergreen shrubs and hollies provide a deep green backdrop for bare branches and snow.

By matching and contrasting the colors of flower and foliage, you can create a sequence of visual backgrounds and accents that changes continuously throughout the year.

# LANDSCAPE PLANT GROUPS

In the pages that follow, you will find the basic landscape plant groups, each with a list of selected types and species suitable to your gardening needs. Check out the individual species for their growth habits, frost hardiness, soil preference and any special requirements for fertilizing and watering.

**Turf and Lawn Grasses—Pgs. 32–37**
Cool and warm season lawn grasses suitable for your area; decorative clumping grasses and extra-hardy grasses for problem areas.

**Vines and Climber Roses—Pgs. 42–45**
Different varieties of vines, climbing by tendrils or clinging by holdposts; training vines on walls, trellises and fences; climber and rambler roses.

**Groundcovers—Pgs. 38–41**
Deciduous and evergreen groundcovers for every landscaping situation; tips on installation and maintenance for different species.

**Seasonal and Perennial Color—Pgs. 46–49**
Annual, biennial and perennial plants for garden color throughout the growing season; choosing between nursery grown annuals and perennials.

**Shrubs—Pgs. 50–55**
Using evergreen and deciduous shrubs in the landscape; selecting shrubs for size, shape and color; feeding, shaping and pruning your shrubs.

**Cactus and Succulents—Pgs. 62–63**
Creating arid country landscapes with cactus and succulents; the basics of cactus and succulent care; using ice plant for flowering groundcover.

**Trees—Pgs. 56–61**
Characteristics of fine-needled conifers and broadleafed evergreen and deciduous trees; ornamental, shade and screen trees suitable for your area.

**Ferns—Pgs. 64–65**
Using woodland ferns in the landscape; soil, sun and water requirements of the most popular ferns.

# TURF AND LAWN GRASSES
## COOL-SEASON GRASSES

## CHOOSING GRASSES

Whether you're installing turf for the first time or renovating an established lawn, careful planning and ground preparation are essential. Many grasses are sensitive to extremes of temperature and rainfall, so select appropriate grasses.

Lawn grasses are generally divided into cool-season and warm-season species; local variations in rainfall, soil type and sun or shade will determine the best species for you. Most varieties are available as seed or sod, but some of the warm-season grasses, such as St. Augustine and Improved Bermuda, are also sold as sprigs or plugs. Seeds are available as straight and blended species, or as mixes developed for optimum pest and disease resistance in particular areas. Seeding is inexpensive but can involve daily watering and considerable maintenance until the lawn is established.

Also decide how much maintenance you want to do—lawns require regular watering, fertilizing and mowing. Every type of grass has different requirements for mowing height, pest control and soil nutrition. Low maintenance lawns using native grasses and groundcovers are increasingly popular, but special decorative grasses can also be used to create variety and color accents within the landscape.

Don't be frightened off. Turfgrasses require regular care and upkeep, but can be easy to maintain.

**Colonial Bentgrass**

*Agrostis tenuis*

Fine-leaved cool-season grass. Browns easily; heavy watering. Mow to 1/4–1 in. Seed, sprig or sod.

**Creeping Bentgrass**

*Agrostis palustris*

Ideal for putting greens; requires low mowing and sandy loam. Poor drought and disease tolerance. Mow to 1/4–1 in. Seed, sprig or sod.

**Kentucky Bluegrass**

*Poa pratensis*

Excellent dark green lawn grass. Steady watering, moderate feeding. Mow to 1 1/2–2 in. Seed, sprig or sod.

## Hard or Sheep's Fescue

*Festuca ovina*

Grows and wears well in hot weather or shade. Disease resistant. Requires little water. Mow 1 1/2 in. high. Seed in fall or spring.

## Red Fescue

*Festuca rubra*

Does well in shade, dry soil. Tolerates acid soil. Mow to 2–3 in. Seed, sprig or sod.

## Annual Ryegrass

*Lolium multiflorum*

Not recommended. Medium- to coarse-leaved annual grass; tends to clump. Heavy watering. Mow to 1 1/2–2 in. Seed or sprig.

## Chewings Fescue

*Festuca rubra commutata*

Shade tolerant, dry soil. Mixes well with Kentucky bluegrass. Mow to 1–2 in. Seed or sprig.

## Tall Fescue

*Festuca arundinacea*

Drought tolerant coarse fescue. Excellent for lawns. Tolerates part shade. New hybrids are selected for finer leaf and compact growth. Mow to 3–4 in. Seed or sprig.

## Perennial Ryegrass

*Lolium perenne*

Coarse, drought tolerant grass. Likes mild winters, cool summers. Mow to 1–2 in. Seed, sprig or sod.

# Turf and Lawngrasses
## Warm-Season Grasses

### Bahiagrass

*Paspalum notatum*

Coarse, fast-growth and easy-care grass. Tolerates shade and drought. Mow to 2–3 in., moderate fertilization. Seed.

### Improved Bermudagrass

*Cynodon dactylon*

Better appearance and performance than common bermudagrass. Mow to 1/2–1 in. Sprigs, plugs or sod.

### Common Bermudagrass

*Cynodon dactylon*

Drought tolerant; needs full sun. Browns in winter in cold climates. Heavy fertilization, mow to 1 in. Sprigs, plugs, sod or seed.

### Buffalograss

*Buchloe dactyloides*

Thin, drought-tolerant grass used in high plains from Texas to Canada; mow to 1 in., browns in winter. Sprigs, plugs or sod.

## Centipedegrass

*Eremochloa ophiuroides*

Hardy, easy-care grass. Tolerates light shade and poor soil. Mow to 2 in. Sprigs, plugs, sod or seed.

## Saltgrass

*Puccinellia distans* 'Fults'

Tolerates saline, alkaline soil where other turfgrasses cannot grow. Seed or sod.

## Seashore Paspalum

*Paspalum vaginatum*

Cool coastal area grass; full sun, drought tolerant. Sold in spring as sod. Mow to 2 in.

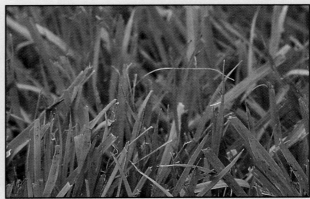

## Zoysiagrass

*Zoysia japonica*

Fine textured warm climate grass, often sold as plugs. Slow growing; mow to 1/2–1 1/2 in. Sprigs, plugs or sod.

## St. Augustinegrass

*Stenotaphrum secundatum*

Good shade grass, tolerates salty soil. Heavy watering, mow to 1 1/2–2 1/2 in. Sprigs, plugs or sod.

# Decorative and Grass-Like Plants

## Reedgrass

*Calamagrostis x acutiflora 'Stricta'*

Tall annual-flowering hybrid reed grass. Full or part sun, damp soil. Zones 5–10.

## Blue Fescue

*Festuca ovina glauca*

Mounds of blue-gray leaves 6–12 in. Good for borders and accents. Zones 4–10.

## Fountaingrass

*Pennisetum alopecuroides*

Dark green decorative grass, grows to 3–4 ft. Foxtail flower spikes. Full sun, well-drained soil. Zones 6–9.

## Blue Oatgrass

*Helictotrichon sempervirens*

Blue-gray clumping grass, grows to 3–4 ft. Needs sun, well-drained soil. Zones 4–10.

## Pampasgrass

*Cortaderia selloana*

Large plumed grass, arching leaves to 8 ft. long, cream-colored plumes 12–20 ft. High maintenance; full sun, rich well-drained sandy soil. Zones 8–10, further north as annual.

## Mondograss

*Ophiopogon japonicus*

Slow-growing evergreen grass, to 6 in. or higher. Spreads by runners, forms sod. Full or part shade, full shade in hot climates. Pale purple summer flowers. Zones 8–10.

## Sea Pink

*Armeria maritima*

Small clumping plant, pink flowers in late spring, summer. 3–4 in. leaves, stems to 1 ft. or more. Fast growing. Zones 4–9.

## Stipa

*Stipa* species

Fine-stemmed feathery grass, various species grow from 3–6 ft. Full sun, well-drained soil. Zones 5–9.

# GROUNDCOVERS

## PLANTING GROUNDCOVERS

For landscapes where turfgrass lawns and flower beds are difficult—hillsides, rocky surfaces, under trees and in overly dry or wet soil—groundcovers are an excellent, low-maintenance alternative. Groundcovers can be almost any durable, low-growing plant that spreads horizontally to form a carpet-like surface; they knit their roots into soil, spread over brick and stone into crevices, and even creep around barriers and borders. Once well established, groundcovers generally require little upkeep.

Groundcovers have a number of important roles in the garden—erosion control, foliage and flower color, weed control and edging. Put them to good use. As a rule, groundcovers should be planted in the spring. Limit access until they are well established. Different groundcover species adapt to most conditions, but good drainage is desirable.

Although groundcovers need less maintenance, they require special care during installation. Select a type suitable to your landscape and buy enough plants to cover the entire area. Loosen the soil to 4–6 in. and check that each plant has a strong root system. Groundcover will spread its vines or send out runners to intertwine with its neighbors in short order.

Until they are established, most groundcovers will need regular watering and fertilization.

**Carpet Bugle**

*Ajuga reptans*

Fast-growing perennial, to 12 in. Deep blue or white flowers in late spring. Subject to disease. Zones 2–10.

**Bearberry, Kinnikinnick**

*Arctostaphylos uva-ursi*

Medium-fast growth to 1 ft. high, spreads to 15 ft. White and pink flowers in early spring, berries in summer. Sun to part shade. Zones 3–9.

**Silver Lace**

*Artemisia* species

Perennial herb, 1–3 ft. tall, with silver leaves and small flowers. Drought resistant and salt tolerant. Plant in well-drained soil and full sun. Zones 3–9.

## Plumbago

*Ceratostigma plumbaginoides*

Nearly evergreen, low mat to 18 in. Blue flowers in summer, fall. Foliage colors with frost. Well-drained, fertile soil. Zones 5–9.

## Winter Creeper

*Euonymus fortunei*

Hardy evergreen vine, trails out to 20 ft. Leaves turn purple in autumn and winter. Zones 4–9.

## Rock Cotoneaster

*Cotoneaster horizontalis*

Medium-fast growth to 3 ft. Pink-white flowers, dark green, herringbone-pattern leaves. Full sun. Zones 4–9.

## Ivy

*Hedera* species

Fast growth, dark green 2–3 in. leaves, will also climb by aerial roots. Moist soil, sun or shade. Zones 5–10.

## Dichondra

*Dichondra repens caroliniensis*

Fast-growing evergreen, up to 1 ft. Low, round-leaf groundcover that tolerates shade. Mow to 1 in. Low maintenance but heavy fertilization. Zones 9–10.

## Plantation Lily

*Hosta* species

Mounding, slow growth to 3 ft. Spike-like lavender to pink bloom in late summer. Part sun or shade, moist soil. Zones 3–9.

# GROUNDCOVERS

## Aaron's Beard

*Hypericum calycinum*

Fast-growing evergreen, up to 1 ft. high. Yellow flowers in late spring, early summer. Sun or shade. Zones 5–10.

## Isotoma

*Isotoma* species

Dainty small leaves of light green and tiny, star-shaped flowers in white, blue or purple, to 1 ft. Zones 8–10.

## Trailing Lantana

*Lantana montevidensis*

Fast-growing evergreen, to 3 ft. high, spreads to 6 ft. Low maintenance. Full sun, little watering. Zones 8–10.

## Creeping Lilyturf

*Liriope* species

Evergreen leaves, medium growth to 10 in. Clumps merge by spreading underground runners. Full or part sun. Zones 6–10.

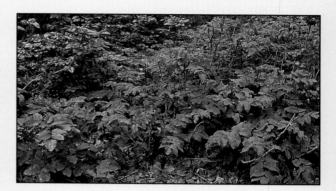

## Oregon Grape

*Mahonia repens*

Thornless evergreen, 3-in. leaves, blue-black berries in fall. Sun to part shade, moderate watering. Zones 5–10.

## Japanese Spurge

*Pachysandra terminalis*

Moderate-growth green foliage evergreen, to 5–10 in. high. Does well in shade, needs regular watering and acid soil. Zones 3–8.

## Moss Phlox

*Phlox subulata*

Matting perennial with semievergreen, needle-like foliage to 6 in. Pink flowers in spring. Sun, well-drained soil. Zones 2–3.

## Santolina

*Santolina chamaecyparissus*

Gray foliage evergreen, medium-growth to 2 ft. high, spreads up to 6 ft. Drought tolerant, small yellow flowers in spring. Zones 7–8.

## Cinquefoil

*Potentilla villosa*

Fast-growing evergreen, to 6 in. high. Sun to part shade in hot climates. Zones 2–8.

## Sedum

*Sedum floriferum*

Slow-growing succulent, to 2 in. Yellow flowers in late spring. Full sun, moderate watering. Zones 4–9.

## Rosemary

*Rosmarinus officinalis*

Medium-fast-growing evergreen, to 2–4 ft high. Fragrant, dark green needles. Blue flowers in early spring. Full sun, well-drained soil. Zones 7–10.

## Dwarf Periwinkle

*Vinca minor*

Fast-growing, hardy trailing evergreen, 2-in. leaves. Blue flowers in spring. Full or part shade, well-drained soil. Zones 5–9.

**41**

## CLIMBING VINES

Vines are one of the most varied and useful plant groups available to the landscape gardener. They can be trained to climb up vertical supports or across arbors and trellises, to cover fences and walls or to create screens providing shade from the sun. There are numerous varieties of foliage, flowering and fruit-bearing vines.

Vining plants are any species of plant that grows by elongating its stems so as to climb vertically or creep horizontally. Vines can climb by a number of methods, from trailing out stems or hooking onto supports with thorns or spikes, to weaving in and out of whatever object presents itself. Some vines set out roots which anchor them onto rocks, branches and trunks, or any surface with holes or cracks. Most vines either twine themselves, clockwise or counter-clockwise, with a slow rotary movement of the growing tip of the stem, or cling with tendrils or stickers that grip or coil around supporting surfaces.

Most vines are warm-weather plants, but some are hardy enough for northern climates. To choose a vine for your landscape, first consider how and where it will climb or creep as it grows—horizontally as a groundcover, or up a trellis as a screen. Vines can be attractive for their foliage alone (ivy), for their flowers (clematis), or for their scent (honeysuckle). Most vines are fairly vigorous and fast-growing plants, but some require special care. A few can be real troublemakers unless they are diligently pruned. One such problem vine, the notorious kudzu (*Pueraria lobata*), grows from 50–75 ft. a year in the moist, hot areas of the Deep South, covering everything in sight.

**Clematis**

*Clematis* species

Fast-growing, deciduous vine, to 10–12 ft. high. White, blue, purple, pink or red flowers bloom spring, summer or fall. Cut to ground in winter. Part shade; moist, well-drained soil. Zones 5–9.

**Honeysuckle**

*Lonicera* species

Fast-growing, hardy vine, train to 10–15 ft. Red, 2-in. flowers in summer. Full sun or part shade, moist but well-drained soil. Zones 5–10.

## Bougainvillea

*Bougainvillea* species

Vertically-climbing by twining stems and thorns, brilliant purple, red, orange or white flowers peak in summer. Full sun, moist soil. Zone 10.

## Wine Grape

*Vitus vinifera*

Deciduous vine with dominant trunk and branch pattern for winter interest. Grows to 50 ft. Vigorous and hardy. Zones 5–10.

## Wisteria

*Wisteria japonica*

Hardy, grows up to 50 ft. high. Strong, woody trunks need good support. Full sun, well-drained soil; shelter from wind. Zones 3–10.

## Boston Ivy

*Parthenocissus tricuspidata*

Highly popular ivy of "Ivy League" to 50 ft. Semi-evergreen. Good fall color, fast grower. Well-drained soil. Zones 5–10.

## Passionflower

*Passiflora* species

Fast-spreading, grows to 20 ft. or more. Good for trellises; showy 3–4 in. flowers. Moist, well-drained sandy loam. Zone 10.

## Star Jasmine

*Trachelospermum jasminoides*

Slow-growing evergreen, twining to 15–20 ft. or more. Fragrant, yellow-white flowers in spring and summer. Moist, well-drained soil; part shade. Zones 9–10.

# CLIMBER AND RAMBLER ROSES

## ROSES IN THE LANDSCAPE

Among ornamental plants, roses are usually thought of as flowering shrubs. They are admired chiefly for their color and fragrance. Roses known as climbers and ramblers can also provide vertical foliage and background color, cover fences, or spread horizontally as a sturdy groundcover.

Most of the so-called climbing roses don't actually cling or grasp to their vertical supports. They need to be trained and tied in order to climb upward on trellises, arbors and fences. True rambler roses, on the other hand, will follow any solid support—train them along arbors, pillars and posts. They make a lovely cover for landscape structures, twining their thorny canes into and around arches and gazebos, gradually assuming their shape.

Many climbing roses bloom only once a season, but also serve as year-round foliage, hedges or groundcovers—their seasonal color is an added bonus.

Rambler roses generally have smaller, clustering flowers—prune them only to remove diseased or damaged canes. Then cut again after blooming is finished for a good color show the following year. Climbers, on the other hand, bloom with larger flowers, once or twice a season, depending on the cultivar type. Prune one-time flowering types after they bloom in the spring, or just before winter dormancy ends for the multiple bloomers.

**Climbing America**

*Warriner, 1976*

Well-formed, large, coral-pink blooms. Flowers have rich, spicy scent and form on new and old wood. Long canes. AARS 1976.

**Climbing Pinata 3996**

*Suzuki, 1978*

Bright yellow and orange-red blooms. Canes grow 6–8 ft. high.

**Climbing Blaze**

*Kallay, 1932*

Most popular climber. Masses of bright red blooms in large clusters form on new and old wood.

44

### Climbing White Dawn

*Longley, 1949*

Constant blooms of clear white, ruffled flowers on a vigorous, disease-resistant plant. Blooms on new and old wood.

### Climbing High Noon

*Lammerts, 1948*

Lemon yellow, large, fragrant flowers set off by shiny green foliage. Disease resistant. Blooms on new and old wood. AARS 1948.

### Climbing Joseph's Coat

*Swim & Armstrong, 1964*

Very popular multicolor climber in shades of pink, red, orange and yellow. Blooms on new and old wood.

### Climbing Blue Girl

*Kordes, 1964*

Sport of parent Blue Girl. Large, fragrant lavender flowers. Vigorous. Blooms on new and old wood.

### Climbing Golden Showers

*Lammerts, 1956*

Masses of fragrant, pure yellow, ruffled flowers. Good climber. Blooms on new and old wood. AARS 1956.

### Climbing Royal Gold

*Morey, 1957*

Deep yellow "Hybrid Tea" blooms with stems long enough to cut. Fragrant. Blooms on new and old wood.

### Climbing Don Juan

*Maladrone, 1958*

Deep, velvety red, 5 in. flowers. Vigorous, very fragrant. Blooms on new and old wood.

### Tempo 3652

*Warriner, 1975*

Bright red flower clusters cover from spring to fall. Bright, dark green foliage. Blooms on new and old wood.

# SEASONAL COLOR

## CONTAINER-GROWN BEDDING PLANTS

When purchasing container-grown plants, you will be choosing between annual, biennial and perennial plants. Annuals are grown from seed, and complete their life cycle within a single growing season. Biennials are also grown from seed one year to flower in the next. Sow your annuals from seed or buy container-grown plants. They are sold in packs, small pots or flats that permit quick and easy installation of flowering borders and beds and allow the composition of color sequences, by moving the pots around before planting.

Perennials are long-term landscaping plants. They return, year after year, to bloom again in the growing season. Once large enough, many can be divided again and again. Most perennials are used in combination with annuals and bulbs to create a continuing, season-long sequence of color in the garden.

Shrubs and trees should also be considered for their seasonal color; note their order of bloom and whether their foliage turns with the seasons when planning the color sequence of the landscape plants around your flower beds. Contrast planting brings out the best in plant color, form and texture, no matter which seasonal color plants you are considering.

**Cosmos**

*Cosmos* species

Annual from 4–6 ft. in height, making excellent borders and massed plantings. 1–2 in. flowers from white to yellow-gold to pink. Full sun, dry soil.

**Coleus**

*Coleus* species

Varigated foliage ranging from green to white and red. Sun to full shade, moist location.

**Marigold**

*Tagetes* species

Bright, ruffled flowers on short or tall stalks bloom until frost. Full sun.

## Periwinkle

*Catharanthus roseus*

Low, mounding growth to 10 in. White or pink flowers in spring and summer. Full sun or part shade in moist soil.

## Impatiens

*Impatiens* species

Dark green leaves; grows to 1–2 ft. with 1 1/2 in. flowers in wide variety of colors. Rich, moist soil, full or part shade.

## Salvia

*Salvia splendens*

Grows from 1–2 ft. high. Bright flower spikes atop attractive leaves. Full sun or part shade.

## Sweet Alyssum

*Lobularia maritima*

Mounding edge plant with white, pink or lavender flowers in summer. Full sun.

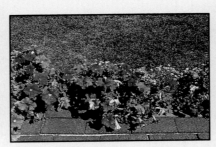

## Petunia

*Petunia x hybrida*

Varieties grow from 10–15 in., showing 2–5 in. early blossoms in all colors. Full sun, sandy well-drained soil.

## Zinnia

*Zinnia elegans*

Popular annual, grows to 2–3 ft. with large, 2–6 in. flowers in all colors. Full sun, rich and well-drained soil. Regular watering and feeding.

## Begonia

*Begonia* species

Grows to 1 ft. with widely varied flowers and foliage color from summer to fall. Semi-sunny, moist sites.

## Geranium

*Pelargonium x hortorum*

Trailing or upright plant to 18 in. high, clusters of flowers in a wide range of colors. Cool climates only. Slightly acid, well-drained soil. Full sun.

## Violas and Pansies

*Viola* species

Perennial grown as annual; 6–8 in. high. Sun or part shade. Needs moist soil.

# PERENNIALS

## Yarrow

*Achillea filipendula* 'Coronation Gold'

Naturalized in some areas, tall herb to 3 ft. Flowers in spring and summer. Full sun in damp, humus-rich soil. Zones 3–9.

## Astilbe

*Astilbe* species

White, pink or bright red stalks of feathery flowers in summer. Full to part sun, moist soils. Zones 4–8.

## Hollyhock

*Alcea rosea*

Heritage flowers with tall spikes of blooms in summer to fall, to 6 ft. Full sun in rich soil. Zones 2–9.

## Bellflower

*Campanula* species

Violet flowers from spring to summer, plants vary from 4 in. to 6 ft. Full or part sun. Zones 3–9.

## Columbine

*Aquilegia* species

Single or double flowers in spring, with graceful foliage to 2 1/2 ft. Full or part sun. Zones 3–9.

## Shasta Daisy

*Chrysanthemum maximum*

A sunny garden classic—flowers with white radiating petals from a bright yellow center reach 6 in. diameter, to 4 ft. Zones 5–9.

## Delphinium

*Delphinium* species

Stalks to 6 ft. tall, purple 2-in. flowers in summer. Full sun, moist, well-drained soil. Zones 3–10.

## Lupine

*Lupinus polyphyllus*

Tall, with spikes of flowers in blue, pink, red, yellow and purple, to 5 ft. Full sun, sandy soils. Zones 4–7.

## Bleeding Heart

*Dicentra eximia*

Native plant to 18 in. tall, with hanging, heart-like flowers from spring to fall. Shady, moist soil. Zones 2–9.

## Poppy

*Papaver* species

Beautiful pastel flowers on tall stalks, to 6 ft. Flowers in spring and summer. Full sun in moist soil. Zones 1–8.

## Daylily

*Hemerocallis* species

Striking trumpets of brightly colored, multiple flowers on stalks from 12–48 in. Adaptable to soil conditions. Full to part sun, moist soils. Zones 3–9.

## Gloriosa Daisy

*Rudbeckia hirta*

Hybrid of wild Black-eyed Susan, blooms in summer and fall with striking flowers on tall stems, to 36 in. Full sun. Zones 3–9.

# SHRUBS

## SHRUBS IN THE LANDSCAPE

Long-lasting and versatile, landscape shrubs can be adapted to almost any garden plan. They serve as flowering plants, foliage color, hedges, edgings and even as screens. Shrubs are low-maintenance plants, requiring only occasional pruning and fertilization unless they are being shaped into formal hedges. Their variety is the key to their versatility—nearly every size, shape, color and texture may be found.

Shrub selection should be done in the early stages of landscape planning. Individual flowering or specimen shrubs should be placed as accents in conspicuous spots, while groups of spreading shrubs can be planted closely together to form dense walls of vegetation around the landscape. Depending on their size and type of foliage, shrubs can give a light, airy feeling to the landscape, or add weight and mass as backdrops and screens. Trained as vertical forms, shrubs become treelike—the larger upright shrubs are often indistinguishable from small trees.

Shrubs can be evergreen or deciduous, flowering or foliage only, low-growing, upright or even climbing. Like trees, shrubs should be planted with a view to their final, mature size and shape.

Many shrubs can be bought or grown as dwarf specimens, and frequent pruning will always control a shrub's final size.

### Abelia

*Abelia grandiflora*

Mounding shrub, grows to 5 ft. or more. Deciduous in northern range. Sun or part shade, well-drained soil. Zones 5–10.

### Dwarf Barberry

*Berberis thunbergii* 'Crimson Pigmy'

Slow-growing deciduous shrub; dense, dark green leaves, yellow flowers. Scarlet color, red berries in fall. Sun to part shade, moist well-drained soil. Zones 4–9.

### Boxwood

*Buxus* species

Upright, hardy evergreen for formal plantings, can grow to 3–4 ft. Sun or part shade, takes shearing. Zones 5–10.

## Heather

*Calluna vulgaris*

Small, narrow-leaved evergreen, grows to 2–3 ft. Purple-pink flowers. Moist, acid soil, full sun. Zones 4–6.

## Camellia

*Camellia Japonica*

Popular evergreen plant, upright to spreading form. Long dark leaves, brilliant flowers. Shade or part-sun, rich acid soil. Zones 7–8.

## Dwarf Hinoki Cypress

*Chamaecyparis obtusa*

Small evergreen, needs pruning to keep to 5 ft. or less. Interesting spreading branch forms. Zones 5–10.

## Dogwood

*Cornus* species

Reddish limbs with showy white flowers that appear in early spring, vivid foliage color in fall. Part shade. Zones 2–8.

## Smokebush

*Cotinus coggygria*

Tall, to 15 ft. or more, with broad, flat leaves and feathery flowers in spring. Good fall color. Full sun. Zones 5–9.

## Cotoneaster

*Cotoneaster* species

Both evergreen and deciduous shrubs, 1–10 ft. White flowers in spring or summer. Full sun, little care. Zones 4–9.

**51**

# SHRUBS

## Daphne

*Daphne* species

Evergreen vase-shaped shrub, grows to 3 ft. or more. Pink flowers in spring. Most species are fragrant. Needs good, slightly alkaline soil. Zones 4–9.

## Veronica

*Hebe* species

Round, low evergreen, grows to 5 ft. Purple, white or pink spiking flowers in summer. Full sun, well-drained soil. Zones 9–10.

## Euonymus

*Euonymus* species

High shrub to 12 ft. with glorious fall color foliage. Full to part sun, moist soil. Zones 3–8.

## Hydrangea

*Hydrangea* species

Medium bush to 5 ft. with large green leaves and masses of flowers in summer. Full to part sun, in moist soil. Zones 5–10.

## Holly

*Ilex* species

Holly grows from 2–20 ft. high. Full sun, part shade. Zones 5–10.

## Juniper

*Juniper* species

Easily trained, low or high shrub with dense, evergreen needle-like foliage. Full sun, does well even in poor soils. Zones 3–9.

## Myrtle

*Myrtus communis*

Aromatic leaves. Dense shrub grows to 8–10 ft. White flowers in summer, berries in fall. Full sun, dry soil. Zones 8–10.

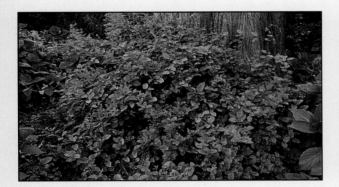

## Honeysuckle

*Lonicera* species

Vine-like hedge shrub, with fragrant flowers, to 15 ft. with support. Red or yellow flowers in summer. Sun. Zones 3–9.

## Heavenly Bamboo

*Nandina domestica*

Upright stalks, evergreen, member of Barberry family, grows to 8 ft. Bright red berries, scarlet foliage in winter. Sun or part shade. Zones 6–10.

## Star Magnolia

*Magnolia stellata*

Upright deciduous shrub or tree to 20 ft. White flowers in spring. Fertile, well-drained soil. Zones 5–9.

# SHRUBS

## Dwarf Ninebark

*Physocarpus opulifolius intermedius*

Dark green, mounding deciduous shrub, grows from 2–5 ft. Small white to pink flowers. Zones 2–8.

## Bird's Nest Spruce

*Picea abies* 'Nidiformis'

Low, dense evergreen, slow-growing to spreading bush. Dwarf form of Norway Spruce. Zones 2–8.

## Cinquefoil

*Potentilla* species

Finely textured foliage with multiple blooms in summer, to 5 ft. Sun in moist soil. Zones 2–8.

## Azalea

*Rhododendron* species

Rounded, spreading deciduous shrub, grows to 4 ft. Part shade, well-drained sandy loam. Zones 4–9.

## Rhododendron

*Rhododendron* species

Dense-leaved plant, provides tall evergreen backdrop to 25 ft. Flowers in summer. Full or part shade, acid soil. Zones 3–9.

## Japanese Rose

*Rosa rugosa*

Spreading, dark-green deciduous shrub, grows to 6 ft. Pink or white flowers in June, large red hips in fall. Hardy to Zone 2–9.

## Spiraea

*Spiraea* x *van houttei*

Graceful arching branches with white flowers, to 6–8 ft. Full sun in moist soils. Zone 4–8.

## Lilac

*Syringa* species

Fragrant deciduous upright, grows to 20 ft. White or purple flowers in early summer. Full sun, any good soil. Zones 3–8.

## Golden Yew

*Taxus baccata* 'Stricta Aurea'

Slow-growing evergreen hedge and edging plant, shears well, grows up to 20 ft. Any well-drained soil. Sun or shade. Zones 6–9.

## Germander

*Teucrium chamaedrys*

Medium-growth evergreen, spreads to 2 ft. or more. Small, deep-purple or white flowers in summer. Full sun or part shade, well-drained soil. Zones 6–8.

## Viburnum

*Viburnum* species

Broad-leaved evergreen or deciduous shrubs to 8 ft. Deeply-veined leaves. White flowers in spring, summer or fall. Colorful fruit. Part shade. Zones 4–9.

# TREES
## *CONIFERS*

### LANDSCAPE TREES

Trees, woody perennial plants growing to heights of 15-20 feet or more, are usually the largest and most dominant element in the landscape garden. Your site may already have an abundance of trees, and new landscapes and new plantings need to be planned carefully. The shape, size and growing habits of a tree will determine whether it is suitable for your site. Once established, trees are difficult to move, as their roots often spread out to two or three times the diameter of their outer branches.

Regardless of its form, learn how far your tree's branches will ultimately extend and situate it accordingly. Keep in mind any overhanging wires or structures, competing plants and shadows to be cast by the mature specimen.

Landscape trees are classified according to type—evergreen or deciduous, broadleaved or conifer—or use—ornamental, shade or screen trees. Most landscape trees will look good whether planted alone, in groups, or in groves, but unusual specimens are better placed by themselves in sites appropriate to their scale and form. Position new trees carefully, using an overhead bubble diagram and an eye-level drawing of mature shapes (see pgs. 18-19).

If you have selected trees suited to your climate zone and site, major soil amendment should not be needed. The trees will adjust to the native soil. Nevertheless, improving drainage and grading before planting can improve a tree's chances. Pruning limbs and branches will often improve a mature tree's appearance.

**Japanese Yew**

*Taxus cuspidata*

Slow dense growth, to 20 ft. high and 20 ft. wide in some varieties. Good for topiary. Sun or shade. Zones 4–8.

**American Arborvitae**

*Thuja occidentalis*

Narrow upright, grows to 60 ft. Full sun. Tolerates wet soil. Zones 2–7.

**Dwarf White Spruce**

*Picea glauca* 'Conica'

Compact pyramidal tree. Slow growing to 7 ft. Short fine needles soft to the the touch. Zones 3–8.

**Monterey Pine**

*Pinus radiata*

Rapid growing with single or multiple trunks, to 60 ft. or more. Full sun in well-drained soil. Zones 8–10.

## Pine

*Pinus* species

Widely varied group of single or multiple-trunk trees with grouped needles, 20–60 ft. or more tall. Full sun. Zones 2–9.

## Colorado Blue Spruce

*Picea pungens*

Rigid, with graceful, open growth to 150 ft. or more. Dense needles circle branches. Full sun in moist, well-drained soil. Zones 4–8.

## Douglas Fir

*Pseudotsuga menziesii*

Huge, with graceful, open growth to 150 ft. or more. Dense needles circle branches. Full sun in moist, well-drained soil. Zones 4–8.

## Western Hemlock

*Tsuga heterophylla*

Rounded upright conical, grows to 100 ft. in cultivation. Needs moist soil. Zones 6–8 in West, 7–8 in East.

## Italian Cypress

*Cupressus sempervirens*

Upright column, dark green, grows to 60 ft. Formal group or row plantings. Zones 7–9.

## Monterey Cypress

*Cupressus macrocarpa*

Irregular or spreading upright, grows to 75 ft. or more. Salt tolerant, does best in seaside breezes. Zones 9-10.

## Redwood

*Sequoia sempervirens*

Narrow upright conical form, fast-growing to 50 ft. in 15 years. Huge at maturity. Zones 8–10.

## Southern Yew

*Podocarpus macrophyllus*

Rounded upright, good for screens, grows to 25 ft. Salt and shade tolerant. Zones 9–10.

# DECIDUOUS AND EVERGREEN TREES

## TREES AND LAWNS

Lawns that contain trees or large shrubs require special attention. By shading the lawn and blocking the rain, trees and shrubs may rob the lawn of needed sunlight and nutrients. Tree leaves, if not raked from the lawn, often provide homes for pests and diseases. Most evergreens and some hardwoods may cause the soil to become too acidic. With a little care and planning, you can have wonderful shade trees and a beautiful lawn, too.

The biggest problem most trees cause for your lawn is shade. Most grasses do not grow as well without full sunlight. One way to solve the problem is to trim the tree, or tall shrub, to allow at least half of the sunlight to filter through. This can be done by carefully selecting the branches to be cut so the tree isn't disfigured. A second step you may want to take in shaded areas is to plant grass types that grow well without full sunlight. You can also reseed under trees using perennial ryegrass.

If you are planning your lawn and landscape, remember that deciduous trees that lose their leaves in winter provide excellent summer shade, but also require more work in autumn. Their leaves should be raked within a few days of falling because they provide pests and lawn diseases with perfect homes. They make good compost.

Almost all trees will form shallow surface roots if their only source of water is your lawn irrigation. Provide deep watering for your trees to prevent these surface roots from making your lawn unsightly.

### Acacia

*Acacia* species

Good shade evergreen, irregular rounded shape, grows to 50 ft. Tolerates drought, poor soil and wind. Yellow flowers in spring. Zones 8–10.

### Maple

*Acer* species

Tall, oval shade tree; grows to 100 ft. Brilliant scarlet to red-orange fall foliage. Moist, well-drained soil. Zones 3–8.

### Japanese Maple

*Acer palmatum*

Small, decorative tree or shrub, to 15 ft. Full sun, part shade in warmer zones. Brilliant foliage, some throughout year. Zones 5–9.

### Madrone

*Arbutus menziesii*

Spreading, rounded ornamental evergreen grows to 100 ft. Needs acid soil. Fruit in fall, winter. Zones 7–9.

## Birch

*Betula* species

Graceful, gray-barked tree with small leaves that turn golden yellow in autumn. Part sun in moist soils, Zones 2–8.

## Dogwood

*Cornus* species

Small flowering ornamental, grows to 30 ft. Blossoms in spring, fruit and scarlet foliage in fall. Zones 4–9.

## Hawthorne

*Crataegus* species

Small, irregular form deciduous ornamental; grows to 25 ft. White flowers in spring, red berries in fall and winter. Zones 4–8.

## Maidenhair Tree

*Ginkgo biloba*

Fan-shaped leaves turn brilliant yellow in fall, to 50 ft. Buy male trees to avoid messy, smelly fruit. Sun. Zones 4–9.

## Redbud

*Cercis* species

Small deciduous ornamental, grows to 25 ft. Sun or part shade. Early spring red or white flowers. Zones 5–9.

## Gum Eucalyptus

*Eucalyptus* species

Narrow, upright aromatic evergreen; grows to 100 ft. Drought tolerant, well-drained soil only. Zones 9–10.

## Thornless Honey Locust

*Gleditsia triacanthos inermis*

Slow growth of plume-like foliage, to 60 ft. Yellow fall color. Full sun in moist soil. Zones 4–9.

# DECIDUOUS AND EVERGREEN TREES

**American Holly**

*Ilex opaca*

Broadleaf evergreen, conical when young, grows to 50 ft. Accepts salt, needs shade and moist soil. Red berries in fall and winter. Zones 4–10.

**American Sweet Gum**

*Liquidambar styraciflua*

Deciduous ornamental and shade tree, grows to 75 ft. Brilliant yellow and scarlet leaves in fall. Tolerates wet soil. Zones 5–9.

**Flowering Crab Apple**

*Malus floribunda*

Small rounded ornamental, grows to 25 ft. Pink-white spring blossoms, fall fruit. Zones 4–7.

**Canary Islands Date Palm**

*Phoenix canariensis*

Ornamental palm, grows to 60 ft. Hardy, fruit in fall, winter. Full sun. Zones 9–10.

**Sweet Bay, Laurel**

*Laurus nobilis*

Triangular broadleaf ornamental, grows to 20–40 ft. Well-drained soil; tolerates drought when mature. Zones 7–9.

**Southern Magnolia**

*Magnolia grandiflora*

Large evergreen, classic ornamental and shade tree, grows to 80 ft. Moist soil, shade. Zones 7–10.

**Olive**

*Olea europaea*

Drought-tolerant ornamental, grows to 30 ft. Fruit in winter, spring; 'Fruitless' cultivar is less messy. Zones 9–10, semihardy Zone 8.

**Weeping Willow**

*Salix* species

Popular spreading willow, grows to 70 ft. Tolerates wetness. Zones 2–8.

## Callery Pear

*Pyrus calleryana 'Bradford'*

Medium-sized triangular ornamental; grows to 50 ft. White flowers in spring, fruit in summer, scarlet-purple foliage in fall. Zones 4–8.

## Oak

*Quercus species*

Large, slow-growing shade tree, to 90 ft. or more tall. Full sun in acidic, well-drained soil. Zones 3–9.

## Pagoda Tree

*Sophora japonica*

Rounded ornamental, grows to 70 ft. Yellow-white flowers in summer; fruit in fall, winter. Zones 4–8.

## Littleleaf Linden

*Tilia cordata*

Handsome, gray bark on quick-growing, upright tree, to 70 ft. Small yellow flowers with rich scent. Full sun. Zones 3–8.

## Oriental Cherry

*Prunus serrulata*

Vase-shaped upright ornamental, grows to 30 ft. Pink flowers in spring, orange foliage color in fall. Full sun, moist soil. Zones 5–9.

## California Live Oak

*Quercus agrifolia*

Rounded evergreen, fast-growing, irregular spreading shapes. Grows to 80 ft. Very drought tolerant. Full sun. Zones 8–10.

## European Mountain Ash

*Sorbus aucuparia*

Deciduous ornamental, grows to 30 ft. Spring blossoms, fall berries. Needs well-drained acid soil. Zones 3–7.

# Cactus and Other Succulent Plants

## Arid Landscapes

Cactus and other succulent plants are natural landscape elements in the hot, arid regions of the southwestern United States, but some hardier types can thrive in more temperate regions if sheltered. The dramatic forms and textures of taller cactus and succulents make striking silhouettes against the earth and sky in open landscapes, while low-growing succulents can serve as ornaments for rocks, walls and crevices.

While desert plants have a well-deserved reputation for being drought-resistant, many are quite sensitive to water, temperature and soil nutrient conditions. They generally need full sun, well-drained soil and balanced soil to grow and flower profusely. Cactus and succulents dry out in very hot climates if their root systems are not well established. Don't assume that these tough-looking plants are immune to insect and soil pests, either—they suffer from insect pests and diseases just like temperate-climate plants.

Ice plant succulents are well suited for groundcovers. Many grow in a wide range of climates. Flowering specimens are adaptable to a wide range of landscape surfaces and require very little soil preparation. Others are ideally suited for loose or sandy soil conditions or for covering steep slopes unsuited for lawns or flower beds. Ice plants are also useful for controlling erosion.

### Century Plant

*Agave americana*

Long, stiff leaves to 6 ft., flower stalk to 30 ft. high with 2 1/2 in. flowers on top. Blooms and dies. Zone 10.

### Aloe

*Aloe nobilis*

Dark green leaves edged with small hooked teeth. Clustered orange-red flowers on 2 ft. stalks in June. Zones 9–10.

### Agave

*Agave* species

Ornamental garden or park plant, spreading swordlike leaves up to 5 ft. long. Green and yellow 2 in. flowers. Needs moist sandy loam, good drainage. Zone 10.

### Saguaro

*Carnegiea gigantea*

Very large columnar form, branches in wild, less frequently in garden. Slow-growing to 60 ft., native of Southwest. Zones 8-9.

**CAUTION**

Never remove native plants from the wild.

## Old Man Cactus

*Cephalocerius senilis*

Long, white, silky hairs conceal spines. The Old Man can grow to 50 ft. Zone 10.

## Hens and Chicks

*Sempervivum* species

Hardy, blue-green rosettes 4–6 in. across, with pink-white flowers in fall or winter. Zones 4–9.

## Cow's Horn

*Euphorbia grandicornis*

Twisting, wavy branches with brown-gray spines, grows to 6 ft., often in pairs. Sun, winter temps. above 50 degrees. Zone 10.

## Prickly Pear

*Opuntia* species

Upright, growing to 4 ft. Flat, oval blue-green pads, pink-red flowers. Any well-drained soil. Zone 4–10.

## Silver Torch

*Cleistocactus strausii*

Columnar, dense silver-white spines, trunk to 2 1/2 in. wide, 6 ft. high. Deep red flowers. Zones 9–10.

## Golden Barrel Cactus

*Echinocactus grusonii*

Popular spherical cactus, reaches 3 ft. or more in diameter. Golden-yellow spines, small red flowers. Zone 8–10.

## Ice Plant

*Lampranthus*

Succulent subshrub with blindingly brilliant large flowers. Plant in full sun. Needs little or no summer water. Zones 8–10.

## Yucca

*Yucca filamentosa*

Stiff, swordlike blue-gray leaves with creamy flowers on tall stems, grows to 6 ft. high. Zones 5–9.

# FERNS

## FERNS IN THE LANDSCAPE

Ferns are versatile landscape plants that make great additions to protected garden areas. They are leafy perennials so their charm lies in the lush green foliage and the light and airy effect of the entire plant. In combination with colorful spreading annuals or perennials, ferns add texture in shady landscape locations.

You can grow ferns alone in bare areas under trees or tall shrubs as attractive, low-maintenance, greenery. Plant larger ferns, with their graceful, arching fronds, against a bare wall or fence. The finely cut leaves make a decorative pattern against a solid backdrop.

Ferns developed long before flowering plants and reproduce in a more primitive way. Instead of seeds, ferns produce spores which are rust-colored and dust-like and grow on the undersides of the fronds. Most ferns spread by underground stems.

The leaves are thin and dry out easily so ferns need a fairly moist environment both to grow well and to reproduce. In addition to fairly constant moisture, ferns need organic matter in the soil and some protection from hot, dry sun. Most types do best in partial shade, with a rich acidic soil (pH5 to 6) and regular water. Add plenty of organic matter when you prepare the soil. Peat moss works best but you can also use compost or leaf mulch.

When you fertilize ferns it is easy to burn the foliage; the best approach is to fertilize only in the spring and summer when the plants are actively growing and then use half the strength recommended on the label. Keep the roots mulched, especially if they begin to show at the soil surface.

It is a good idea to groom ferns occasionally, cutting out dead and scraggly fronds. This encourages the lush, green look that ferns add to a garden setting.

**Maidenhair Fern**

*Adiantum pedatum*

Reaches 24 in. in height. Full shade. Deciduous. Zones 3–8.

**Lady Fern**

*Athyrium filix-femina*

Reaches 3 ft. Wide, sharply cut fronds make good detail plant. Likes partial sun, woods soil, some lime. Deciduous. Zones 4–9.

## Japanese Holly Fern

*Cyrtotomium falcatum*

Stiff fronds reach 2 1/2 ft. in length. Evergreen. Zones 9–10.

## Ostrich Fern

*Matteuccia pennsylvanica*

Reaches 5 ft. or more in length. Likes rich, loamy soil. Deciduous. Zones 3–7.

## Hedge Fern

*Polystichum setiferum*

Low-growing fern with spreading finely-cut fronds make for a lacy plant. Regular summer water. Evergreen. Zones 7–10.

## Tasmanian Tree Fern

*Dicksonia antarctica*

Part or full shade. Handsome large woody trunk to 5 ft. Evergreen. Zones 9–10.

## Polypody Wall Fern

*Polypodium vulgare*

Grows to 10 in. fronds to 18 in. Full or part shade. Evergreen. Zones 3–9.

## Chain Fern

*Woodwardia* species

Found wild from Nova Scotia to Florida, grow to 2 ft. Partial sun. Evergreen. Zones 5–9.

## Woodfern

*Dryopteris* species

Found in wild from northeast U.S. to Arkansas. Grows 2–2 1/2 ft. high. Full or part shade. Deciduous. Zones 3–9.

## Royal Fern

*Osmunda regalis*

Grows to 6 ft. Likes shade, needs moist acid soil to thrive. Deciduous. Zones 3–8.

# LANDSCAPES OVER TIME

## PLANNING LANDSCAPES THAT LAST

After you've designed your landscape and selected your plants, the job of planning is still not complete. Visualize how your landscape will look years down the road simply by imagining what would happen if you let nature take over. Native plants begin to reappear wherever they are not kept out; perennials spread and bunch out; young shrubs and trees grow steadily until they reach maturity. As screen and shade trees grow to full size, shade-loving plants will emerge below them and sun-loving plants will disappear.

All of your plants, native and cultivated, are subject to the natural cycle of growth, change and renewal in the landscape. In the best-planned gardens, the original choice of landscape plants works within a steadily developing environment of vegetation and new specimens. With time, hedges take shape, groundcovers spread and form a mat, and screen shrubs and trees close and intertwine their branches. Slow-growing shrubs and trees may take many years to reach the size you visualized in your landscape plan, so buy the largest specimens you can afford and place them far enough apart to not crowd each other.

Many landscape plants and most lawns eventually reach the end of their lifecycle and require renewal or replacement. If you plan your landscape wisely and maintain it well, however, you will get many years of use and enjoyment from your original plantings.

Bareroot Maple (*Acer* species)

Boxwood (*Buxus* species)

Lilyturf (*Liriope* species)

After One Year

After Five Years

67

# PREPARING TO PLANT

Plant border and edging

Turfgrass

Water service

Topsoil

Subsoil

Roots

68

# CONDUCTING A SOIL TEST

Soil tests measure the amount of nutrients your garden soil has available for your plants, and tell you which fertilizers you need to add for good growth and heavy flowering. You can test soil for many things, but the four basic soil tests are for chemical content—nitrogen, phosphorus, potassium—and pH (acidity or alkalinity).

Nitrogen (N) is needed to produce leaf growth and good chlorophyll. Phosphorus (P) promotes growth of root systems, and stimulates flower and seed formation. Potassium or potash (K) carries carbohydrates throughout the entire plant, building strength and resistance to disease. The pH test measures the overall acidity or alkalinity of the soil.

Mark the location of each soil sample if you are testing a large landscape area. For smaller gardens, mix several samples together to obtain an average sample. Send the sample or samples to a nearby agricultural extension or soil lab. You'll need to be able to properly interpret the results. N, P and K test results are usually expressed as the percentages of nitrogen, phosphorus and potassium fertilizer needed. Fortunately, these percentages are also the three numbers found on the labeling of most fertilizers.

Your pH test result will translate into the amount of lime or sulfur needed to bring the soil back into the desired range. You can actually fine-tune the soil's pH to your plants' individual requirements. For example, most turfgrasses prefer neutral to slightly acid soil (pH 6.5–7.0), ferns like more acidic soil (pH 5.0–6.0). Familiarize yourself with the basics of soil structure and composition before applying fertilizers, lime or sulfur, so you'll know how much soil to turn over for the best results.

# PLANTING SMALL LANDSCAPE PLANTS

Smaller plants, groundcovers and container-grown shrubs can all serve as a quick means to fill in bare areas in the landscape. A little extra care before planting will help them grow and spread rapidly. Take care to water and fertilize plants as needed while they are getting established.

## Groundcovers

**First** Clear soil surface, turn soil to 1 ft. if possible. Spread layer of organic compost over surface, turn into soil.

**Then** Rake level, water to settle soil. Set plants out in staggered rows. Dig holes with trowel or shovel. Loosen roots, place in holes.

**Last** Refill the holes halfway, water to settle, finish filling. Water regularly, soaking roots and avoiding foliage, until established.

## Transplants

**First** Dig holes twice as wide and deep as plants, loosen soil and mix with organic compost and all-purpose fertilizer.

**Then** Remove plants from container, pushing from bottom. Cut any encircling roots, loosen rootball. Place plant in hole, position to ground level.

**Last** Fill with improved soil, firm soil around plant. Water well, reposition plants if necessary.

## Containers

**First** Dig hole twice as wide and deep as container, set aside topsoil on tarp. Mix topsoil with organic compost.

**Then** Place soil in bottom of hole to height where plant will be level or just above ground level. Remove shrub carefully from container, holding by rootball.

**Last** Place shrub in hole, position. Fill halfway with soil, water well to soak rootball. Fill and firm soil. Build water basin at edge of rootball.

# PLANTING LARGE LANDSCAPE PLANTS

Large plants and trees act as backdrops, screens or walls in your garden. These woody plants may be purchased either bare-root or container-grown. Young bare-root trees appear in stores near planting time—it differs for each climate area. Older, container-grown trees are available all year. Choose bare-root or container-grown plants by your plan and budget.

## Bare-Root Plantings

**First**  Prune away any damage or disease. Dig hole 6 in. beyond roots' width and height at old soil line.

**Then**  Mix 0–10–0 fertilizer with soil from hole. Mound soil under roots until the soil line is 1 in. above ground.

**Last**  Press roots to firm soil. Backfill halfway. Settle with water, allow to seep in. Finish fill, mound soil basin.

## Container Plantings

**First**  Lay tree on side, loosen rootball with trowel. Moisten. Slide container from ball. Avoid pulling trunk.

**Then**  Cut any circling roots with knife. Dig hole 6 in. wider than rootball at depth equal to old soil line.

**Last**  Add 4 oz. 0–10–0 fertilizer to native soil. Hold rootball, position soil line at ground surface. Fill and water.

## Boxed Specimen Trees

**First**  Transport to site. Dig hole 1 ft. larger than box. Dismantle box with pry bar and remove. Cut circling roots.

**Then**  Hold tree by rootball, not trunk. Slide into hole without lifting or breaking rootball. **Caution**: *very heavy!*

**Last**  Level to soil surface. Backfill around rootball, mound basin around tree. Fertilize with 0–10–0, water.

# BASIC PRUNING AND LANDSCAPE CARE

Caring for the landscape is a year-round task. Some plants require special maintenance at particular times, while others need only periodic care. Trees and shrubs often require very little help beyond occasional pruning; many evergreen trees rarely need upkeep. Most other trees need regular winter inspection and pruning. Cut fruit trees back about one-quarter while dormant in January or February. Deciduous shade trees may need pruning of limbs in late autumn or winter. Late autumn and early winter are the best times to clean up soil surfaces and remove debris.

In spring, prune your deciduous and evergreen flowering shrubs. Cut back stems and pinch off shoots to encourage spring and summer blossoms. Pinch evergreen flowering shrubs back to shape in late spring—never prune them after mid-summer. Prune deciduous flowering shrubs to shape after blooms fade—trim back old stems and branches from the center of the plant in late summer.

Major pruning of evergreen hedges and screens should wait until plants are dormant. Early fall is the time to prune sugar maple, magnolia and walnut trees; most other deciduous trees can be pruned safely throughout the dormant season.

Check with your local nursery about the need to spray any trees or shrubs that need winter dormant oil and anti-dessicants to prevent drying. Winterize roses and other delicate plants with straw, burlap or other coverings in cold climates.

## Pruning Deciduous Trees and Shrubs

**First** Prune away dead or damaged canes, cutting close to the base at a 45° angle. Cut weak or dead stems back to junction with canes.

**Next** Thin any crossing branches and stems with shears or saw. Light will reach inner branches and leaves to promote growth.

**Last** Cut back 1/4–1/3 of new growth for shape, using pruning shears; make cuts above outside buds so new stems grow away from trunk.

## Hybrid Tea Rose Annual Pruning

**First** Use lopping shears to remove any dead, weakened or diseased branches. Cut back to junction of branch.

**Next** Cut healthy canes back at 45° angle, 1/4–1/2 in. above outside bud. Prune for shape, nipping off tips.

**Last** Remove any suckers from the rootstock. Water.

## Shaping Fine-Leaved Hedges

**First** Cut away dead branches in front of smaller branches. To thin, reach inside outer foliage with pruning shears and cut side branches.

**Next** For formal hedges, set a string between stakes as a guide to the desired height. Let plant grow to string.

**Last** Using hedge shears, trim the foliage wider at the bottom than at the top, or round off at the top.

# LANDSCAPING TOOLS

**Hand broadcast spreader**

**Hand pruning shears**

**Bow rake**

**Shovel**

**Lopping shears**

**Pruning saw**

**Drop or broadc spreader**

The Lawncrafter

**String trimmer**

**Lawn roller**

**Spading fork**

Leaf rake

Rope extension lopper/saw

Electric hedge trimmer

Hoe

Bow saw

Water hose

Barrow or cart

Power mower

77

# BIBLIOGRAPHY AND INDEX

# BOOKS AND ARTICLES FOR FURTHER INFORMATION

Ball, Jeff and Liz. *Rodale's Landscape Problem Solver: A Plant-by-Plant Guide.* Emmaus, Pennsylvania: Rodale Press, 1989.

Bruce, Hal. *How to Grow Wildflowers and Wild Shrubs in Your Garden.* New York: Alfred A. Knopf, 1976.

Gottehrer, Dean M. *Natural Landscaping.* New York: E.P. Dutton/Sunrise, 1979.

Hanner, M. Michael. "Garden Lighting: Illumination for Safety and Enjoyment." *Fine Gardening,* May/June 1991, p. 66.

Hay, Roy, and Synge, Patrick M. *The Color Dictionary of Flowers and Plants for Home and Garden.* New York: Crown Publishers, 1982.

Hoshizaki, Barbara Joe. *Fern Growers Manual.* New York: Alfred A. Knopf, 1975.

Innes, Clive. *The Complete Handbook of Cacti and Succulents.* New York: Van Nostrand Reinhold, 1981.

Nehrling, Arno and Irene. *The Picture Book of Annuals.* New York: Arco, 1977.

Stephenson, Ashley. *The Garden Planner.* New York: St. Martin's Press, 1981.

"Stone, Gravel, Earth and Wood..." *Sunset Magazine,* February 1990, p. 130.

*Western Garden Book.* Menlo Park, California: Sunset Publishing, 1990.

Taylor, Norman. *Taylor's Guide to Groundcovers, Vines & Grasses.* Boston: Houghton Mifflin, 1987.

Taylor, Norman. *Taylor's Guide to Trees.* Boston: Houghton Mifflin, 1987.

"Training Your Own Topiary." *Southern Living,* February 1991, p. 42.

Wirth, Thomas, with Jay Howland. *The Victory Garden Landscape Guide.* Boston: Little Brown and Company, 1984.

Wyman, Donald. *Shrubs and Vines for American Gardens.* New York: Macmillan, 1969.

# A Note From
# NK Lawn and Garden Co.

For more than 100 years, since its founding in Minneapolis, Minnesota, NK Lawn & Garden has provided gardeners with the finest quality seed and other garden products.

We doubt that our leaders, Jesse E. Northrup and Preston King, would recognize their seed company today, but gardeners everywhere in the U.S. still rely on NK Lawn & Garden's knowledge and experience at planting time.

We are pleased to be able to share this practical experience with you through this ongoing series of easy-to-use gardening books.

Here you'll find hundreds of years of gardening experience distilled into easy-to-understand text and step-by-step pictures. Every popular gardening subject is included.

As you use the information in these books, we hope you'll also try our lawn and garden products. They're available at your local garden retailer.

There's nothing more satisfying than a successful, beautiful garden. There's something special about the color of blooming flowers and the flavor of home-grown garden vegetables.

We understand how special you feel about growing things—and NK Lawn & Garden feels the same way, too. After all, we've been a friend to gardeners everywhere since 1884.